CLEVELAND EMOTIONAL HEALTH

PROMOTING DISTINGUISHED
MENTAL HEALTH COUNSELING

Geneseo, N.Y.
clevelandemotionalhealth.com

ISBN Paperback: 979-8-9906284-2-7
ISBN Electronic: 979-8-9906284-3-4

Library of Congress Control Number: 2024914466

Disclaimer:
The content of this book is for informational purposes only and is intended to furnish readers with general information on matters that you may find to be of interest. The information that is provided in this book is not intended to replace or serve as a substitute for business, legal, ethical, or professional advice. The information that is provided in this book is not intended to replace or serve as a substitute for mental health treatment, medical treatment, or advice. As the reader of this book, you understand that the information contained in this book is not intended as a substitute for consultation or treatment with a licensed medical or mental health professional. Please consult with your own mental health counselor/therapist for your mental health needs. The reading and use of this book implies your acceptance of this disclaimer.

Printed in the United States of America.

CONTENTS

~ 1 ~

INSIDE THE AUTHOR'S MIND

Similar to my other practice-informed mental health books, *Cultivating Gratitude, Gratefulness, and Graciousness* serves as an extension of the discussions I have with many of my patients during counseling sessions. These books are carefully crafted to address the challenges and concerns commonly encountered in counseling, offering practical insights and solutions to support your journey toward authenticity, empowerment, and healing.

My mental health philosophy centers on minimizing unnecessary suffering, embracing strengths, practicing self-kindness, shifting perspective, finding meaning, and establishing essential boundaries to honor your authentic self. These principles guide my approach to mental health and well-being. By developing a mindset focused on minimizing unnecessary suffering, connecting to your intuitive nature, and prioritizing your health, this book on cultivating the '3Gs'—gratitude, gratefulness, and graciousness—will assist you, the seeker, in making the healthy changes you desire to reach your mental health goals.

Drawing on my background as a private practitioner, along with my master's and Ph.D. Education in Counseling and Counseling Education, and a lifelong commitment to continuing education, I have distilled key therapeutic concepts and strategies into this engaging and interactive book format. This book is designed to help you develop a deeper understanding of yourself, of others, and to cultivate a lifelong practice of gratitude, gratefulness, and graciousness.

By practicing gratitude and gratefulness, you will learn to appreciate the abundance in your life and acknowledge the kindness and generosity of those around you. Embracing graciousness enables you to purposefully extend kindness, empathy, generosity, and understanding towards others, creating a society where harmony and compassion can thrive.

The cultivation of gratitude, gratefulness, and graciousness—the "3Gs"—encourages a deeper sense of connection and fulfillment, bringing joy and delight to both your personal and interpersonal experiences.

I have designed this interactive book to accompany you on a personal journey towards better connectedness. It is divided into sections to facilitate further engagement with the process and your goals. Therefore, it is important to allow yourself time and space to avoid rushing through the prompts and practices. If, while going through this process, you notice your internal negative critic becoming active and interfering with your journey toward self-improvement, take a moment to pause. This pause will allow you to observe yourself, quiet the critic, and reconnect with your intuitive self—your soul.

That being said, feel free to engage with this book in any way that suits your preferences; there is no wrong approach. However, actively participating in the various exercises provided is highly beneficial promoting focus and being present.

Expressive writing, coloring, and drawing can help you access your thoughts, emotions, and intuition more effectively. Utilizing the spaces provided for personal expression can help you develop valuable insights, compassion, and peaceful fulfillment.

~ 2 ~
CREATIVE ENERGY

Throughout this book, you will discover numerous pages devoted to exercises aimed at cultivating the 3Gs. These exercises primarily involve writing, supplemented by coloring and drawing activities. No particular skill level is required in these areas, as these exercises are designed for personal exploration and, as stated previously, without the use of the negative internal critic.

Studies have shown that engaging in writing, coloring, and drawing helps you connect with the present moment. When you are truly present, you are not preoccupied with regrets about the past or anxieties about the future. Instead, you are fully engaged with whatever you are doing or whomever you are with. The practice of being mindfully present prevents unnecessary suffering and allows space for inner peace and contentment.

"The present moment is where your true and authentic existence lies"
~ Eckhart Tolle, spiritual teacher

In my counseling practice, I often discuss the distinction between negative and positive energy states. Positive energy states are characterized by experiences that provide a sense of meaning and joy, feeding your soul and fueling your vitality. Positive energy is transformative, uplifts your mood, and can make life feel worthwhile.

However, most anything that you do to create or enhance positive and adaptive energy often requires effort and work on your part. Negative or harmful energy states, on the contrary, thrive on self-deprecation and others' misfortunes and weaknesses. Contrary to creative energy states, this pervasive energy requires little effort and can trap you in an addictive cycle of envy, unhappiness, and unnecessary suffering.

Negative energy states (see chapter 3) also have an addictive quality and typically begins with getting a "high" but ultimately drains your energy, leaving you feeling depleted, overwhelmed, anxious, depressed, and filled with self-loathing. By understanding and discerning the difference between these contrasting energy states, it allows you greater awareness and agency over your emotional experiences, enabling a deeper sense of meaning.

Interactive Exercises

The interactive exercises in this book are designed to shift your brain from negative energy to more positive and creative states. They include guided writing prompts, mandala-inspired coloring activities, and various methods for expression through drawing. These exercises can also be highly effective in promoting neurological and emotional transformations.

Writing ~ Ancient Stoic philosophers such as Seneca, Epictetus, and Marcus Aurelius emphasized the importance of journaling and writing as a means to cultivate wisdom, mindfulness, and emotional resilience. The practice of writing is considered a meditative experience that encourages individuals to express their deepest thoughts and emotions without judgment or shame.

The writing you engage in within this book is a private experience that plays a vital role in improving your mental health by providing an outlet for self-expression and emotional processing. Through the prompted writing exercises, you will navigate and articulate self-expression, track behavioral patterns, recognize emotional triggers, and determine necessary changes to enhance your well-being.

Coloring ~ Coloring has a rich history that spans millennia, originating from ancient civilizations like Egypt, and evolved from medieval illuminated manuscripts to printed coloring books in the 17th century. The Renaissance period further advanced coloring techniques, influencing artists like Leonardo da Vinci and Michelangelo. By the 19th century, coloring books became educational tools, teaching children various subjects through engaging illustrations. In the 20th century, coloring gained widespread popularity, with adult coloring books emerging as a therapeutic tool for present-moment mindfulness and relaxing tension in the body.

Coloring serves as a therapeutic activity that enables you to tap into your creativity, release physical tension, and become more present in the moment. Engaging in coloring activates various parts of the brain, encouraging focus and concentration while offering a meditative channel for colorful self-expression.

"Coloring mandalas can be a particularly powerful meditative practice. They have been used for centuries as a way to connect with the inner self and promote spiritual growth."
~ Carl Jung, Psychologist

**Revered mixed media artist Brooke Schery praises this book, in addition to *The Four Essential Pillars of Boundary Setting*, for its ability to instill confidence in herself, her creativity, and her art. Brooke advocates for the use of a diverse array of art supplies, including colored pencils, crayons, ballpoint pens, gel pens, and watercolor markers, for coloring and drawing within this book. According to

Brooke, these tools are optimal for minimizing the risk of bleed-through onto the book's other pages.

Drawing ~ You will notice several blank pages placed throughout this book. These pages are for you to draw or sketch, allowing you to express what is deep within your soul in the present moment. After drawing, take time to reflect and contemplate the meaning it brings forward for you in a kind and compassionate way, without judging yourself or the process.

The purpose of the drawing exercises is that they serve as a powerful tool for interpreting, expressing, and connecting with your emotions and thoughts. When approached without self-criticism, drawing becomes a conduit for exploring the depths of your inner world, allowing you to confront and understand the conflicts or feelings that may be causing you distress.

By engaging in drawing as a creative process, you open up space for reflection and introspection, enabling you to identify any patterns, underlying issues, and authentic strengths. Drawing can serve as a therapeutic outlet, providing a non-verbal means of processing complex emotions and experiences.

Writing, coloring, and drawing collectively serve as powerful tools for promoting gratitude, gratefulness, and graciousness. Through reflection, emotional expression, connection, relaxation, and empowerment, these activities enrich daily life and balanced existence. Moreover, the efforts of any creative self-connection can lead to long-lasting positive effects such as an optimistic outlook, a healthier mindset, and the satisfaction of a life well lived. Embrace and enjoy the process!

WARNING

The content of the upcoming chapter, "Harmful Energy," may have the potential to evoke intense emotions, including feelings of overwhelm, arousal of past traumas, and even anger. Please proceed with caution. If at any point reading this next chapter becomes too overwhelming, feel free to skip it or any sections within it. It is highly recommended that you reach out to your mental health provider for support in navigating any pain or trauma that may arise while engaging with this thought-provoking material.

~ 3 ~

HARMFUL ENERGY

Lacking in the 3Gs—gratitude, gratefulness, and graciousness—can significantly harm your mental health. When you fail to cultivate these qualities, you risk living in a disconnected relationship with yourself, thereby straining relationships with others. There are various ways in which you can unconsciously undermine your 3G practice, usually experienced as perpetuating negative thought patterns and behaviors that obstruct your peace, joy, and contentment. While this book aids in cultivating your creative energy using a variety of 3G practices, the next several pages identify some common types of harmful energy states which likely originated from external influences during childhood. **See warning on the previous page.**

Complaining is an addictive habit and refers to frequently expressing dissatisfaction or grievances in a maladaptive manner. Often times people complain without seeking constructive solutions or taking proactive steps to address the underlying issues. This habit leads to a cycle of negativity, perpetuating feelings of discontentment and frustration, straining relationships, and preventing growth and learning opportunities. It is important to know the difference between stating a viewpoint and complaining. Ask yourself: Is my complaining helpful? Does it change anything?

"What you're supposed to do when you don't like a thing is change it. If you can't change it, change the way you think about it. Don't complain."
~ Maya Angelou.

Blaming or blame-shifting is a negative energy state that entails not accepting responsibility for the part you play in contributing to your own suffering. It is essential to recognize your agency in shaping your experiences and to take ownership of your actions and their consequences. Otherwise, you risk relinquishing control over your life's trajectory, allowing external factors to dictate your fate. By acknowledging the role you play in shaping your reality, you empower yourself to make intentional choices and pursue paths aligned with your values and aspirations. However, failing to take ownership of your actions leads to perpetual blame and victimhood, trapping you in a state of helplessness and a fixed mindset.

"In the long run, we shape our lives, and we shape ourselves. The process never ends until we die. And the choices we make are ultimately our own responsibility."
~ Eleanor Roosevelt

Helplessness, a destructive energy, can trap you in a cycle of victimhood, hampering your ability to cultivate the 3Gs. This mindset creates a sense of powerlessness and resignation, preventing you from taking proactive steps to change your perspective, improve situations, and overcome challenges. When you succumb to feelings of helplessness, you relinquish agency over your life, attributing your circumstances solely to external forces. Consequently, helplessness breeds negativity, bitterness, and resentment, preventing you from recognizing and appreciating the joys and delights in your life.

Moreover, a victim mentality can wear on your relationships, as you feel sorry for yourself and seek sympathy or external validation rather than assuming responsibility for necessary changes in your perspective and behaviors.

"Helplessness is not an inherent trait, but a learned response to adversity. By shifting from a victim mindset to one of empowerment, individuals can transform their lives and cultivate resilience."
~ Martin Seligman, Positive Psychologist

Vengefulness is a deep-seated desire for retaliation or revenge against those perceived to have wronged you. It can manifest as a desire to inflict harm or suffering on others. While seeking revenge may provide temporary satisfaction and is highly energizing, it ultimately perpetuates a cycle of hostility, preventing you from developing deep, intimate relationships with yourself and others. Dwelling on chronic feelings of anger, resentment, and bitterness associated with vengefulness leads to isolation, low self-worth, and a strong sense of not belonging.

"Holding on to anger is like grasping a hot coal with the intent of throwing it at someone else; you are the one who gets burned."
~ Siddhartha Gautama

Gossip is the act of degrading others by spreading rumors based on unsupported assumptions, often fueled by envy, insecurity, or a misguided sense of superiority. It infiltrates lives like a pervasive virus spreading negative energy and toxicity wherever it goes. Gossip corrodes trust, sows discord, and creates an atmosphere of suspicion, fear, and retaliation.

Gossip engenders a culture of judgment and condemnation, where individuals are reduced to mere objects of speculation and ridicule. Moreover, gossip erodes the bonds of friendship, especially in small communities, replacing genuine human connection with shallow and untrustworthy alliances based solely on shared disdain.

Being the target of gossip promotes anxiety, isolation, and insecurity, and leads one to wonder who might be talking behind their back. For the gossiper, gossip acts like a drug, stimulating dopamine levels, creating a craving for more, despite its side effects, which include low self-worth, chronic negative energy, and a deficit of genuine connection and belonging.

"Strong minds discuss ideas, average minds discuss events, weak minds discuss people."
~ Socrates

Drama is the consequence of complex and often unconscious behavior that revolves around creating negative environments. Drama feeds off the negative energy it generates. It is a phenomenon deeply rooted in human psychology, where individuals find themselves entangled in repetitive cycles of reliving past grievances or anxiously anticipating future scenarios, all while behaving as if these events are happening in the present moment.

What's intriguing is that those caught up in drama often fail to recognize it for what it is, largely due to the addictive nature of the energy it generates. This addiction to drama can be so potent that individuals may deny its existence, downplay its significance, normalize it, or minimize it.

16

In essence, drama becomes not just a behavior but a manifestation of the ego's insatiable need for validation, attention, and control. *"Negative people need drama like oxygen. Stay positive, it will take their breath away."*
~ Unknown

Gaslighting is a form of psychological manipulation that occurs over an extended period, leaving the victim questioning the validity of their thoughts, their reality, and if their recollections are accurate. This insidious tactic typically leads to confusion, loss of confidence and self-worth, as well as a victim questioning their emotional and mental stability. Gaslighting is executed gradually, with the abuser subtly undermining the victim's reality, causing them to dismiss each instance as an anomaly. This gradual erosion of the victim's sense of self makes it challenging for them to recognize the manipulation until it is way too deeply entrenched.

Gaslighting is not confined to romantic relationships; it can occur in any dynamic. Perpetrators find victims who are likely to be dependent on them, such as a parent-child relationship or any familial-type relationships. Gaslighting can also be encountered in a toxic work environment or used as political propaganda. The abuser may exploit their position of trust to distort the victim's perception of reality and assert dominance. One common gaslighting technique involves the abuser discrediting others, labeling them as deceitful or unstable, while positioning themselves as the sole arbiter of truth. This tactic serves to isolate the victim, leaving them reliant on the gaslighter for validation and guidance. As a result, victims, especially children, may internalize the gaslighter's narrative, doubting their own experiences and sacrificing their autonomy in the process.

Missing the signs of the negative energy associated with gaslighting entails ignoring and contradicting one's intuitive nature. Cultivating the 3Gs can help you tune into your intuitive nature—your soul.

"Kindness is the language which the deaf can hear and the blind can see."
~ Mark Twain

Envy and Jealousy ~ Both envy and jealousy are harmful energies rooted in negative emotions such as insecurity, inadequacy, and fear. Left unchecked, they can poison relationships and erode self-worth. When consumed by envy or jealousy, your judgment becomes clouded, your perceptions become distorted, and your ability to appreciate your worthiness and accomplishments becomes impeded. Moreover, these emotions often lead to destructive behaviors, such as verbal and emotional abuse, that damage highly valued interpersonal connections.

Oftentimes envy and jealousy are used interchangeably. However, envy typically arises when someone desires something possessed by another person—whether it is their possessions, qualities, achievements, or relationships. It involves feelings of resentment or discontent towards another's perceived advantage or success.

On the other hand, jealousy involves more than two people, where one feels threatened by the attention, affection, or perceived advantages bestowed upon someone else. It is an intense emotional reaction characterized by feelings of insecurity, fear, and resentment, typically triggered by the perceived threat of losing something valuable to a third party.

Jealousy can manifest in possessiveness, suspicion, and hostility towards both the perceived rival and the person or situation at the root of the jealousy.

Typically, excessive jealousy stems from a deep-seated fear of abandonment, inadequacy, or loss of control, resulting in complex interpersonal dynamics and difficulties in understanding and addressing one's self-avoidance tendencies. Self-avoidance tendencies include avoiding facing one's own thoughts, emotions, or issues.

Both envy and jealousy can be destructive because these energies breeds bitterness and a sense of inadequacy within oneself. They often lead to negative thoughts and behaviors, such as gossiping, undermining others, or feeling a sense of injustice. Envy and jealousy can also cause inner turmoil, as you focus on what you lack rather than appreciating your strengths, gifts, and accomplishments.

Self-Righteousness is an attitude and belief characterized by an energizing sense of moral superiority, wherein the individual regards their own beliefs, actions, or affiliations as inherently more virtuous than those of others. Such individuals often display intolerance towards opinions and behaviors they perceive as less virtuous.

Self-righteousness can lead to feelings of arrogance, judgment, and a distorted sense of supremacy. This halts open mindedness, learning, personal growth, and empathy because you are closed off to alternative perspectives and unwilling to acknowledge your own faults or shortcomings.

In your relationships, self-righteousness can strain communication and create conflict, as you impose your beliefs and standards onto others, leading to their resentment and alienation. It can also impede your ability to compromise and collaborate, making it difficult to maintain gainful employment or productive business operations and connections.

"Empathy is seeing with the eyes of another, listening with the ears of another, and feeling with the heart of another."
~ Alfred Adler, The School of Individual Psychology

Temper Tantrums—often referred to as anger management problems—occur when someone reacts with anger or rage because things are not going their way. Unlike anger, which responds to real threats in real time, temper tantrums are exaggerated reactions to not getting one's way. These outbursts are a type of distancing behavior used to avoid any arising emotions related to pain, shame, or fear that seem too overwhelming.

These emotional explosions can also be triggered by feelings of discomfort, disappointment, or an inability to communicate effectively. Temper tantrums can lead to destructive behaviors, such as yelling, hitting, or throwing objects, which can cause physical or emotional harm to those involved. The negative energy of impulsive and unpredictable outbursts strains relationships, making it difficult to resolve conflicts or communicate calmly. This results in chaos, distress, abuse, and discord rather than constructive solutions or positive outcomes.

Worrying is a universal human experience characterized by becoming preoccupied with the potential for detrimental future events or outcomes. It generates a significant amount of maladaptive energy, leading to feelings of anxiety, fear, and distorted beliefs. When you worry, you essentially dwell in a future that has not yet occurred and may never come to pass, causing chronic, addictive, and unnecessary suffering.

However, this habit of worrying does not have the power to alter the outcome of the situation. Instead, it exacerbates matters by clouding judgment, impairing decision-making abilities, and disrupting your capacity to stay grounded in the present moment. Excessive worrying has the potential to become addictive, leading to a disconnect from your loved ones and models detrimental behavioral patterns for future generations, as they likely were modeled for you.

"Worrying is like paying a debt you don't owe. I have spent most of my life worrying about things that have never happened."
~ Mark Twain

Wishing ~ Living in a state of wishing for things or people to be different than they are can generate a significant amount of harmful energy and limit your ability to accept the reality of your situation. When you constantly find yourself wishing for people or things to be different, it leads to a disconnection with reality and a profound sense of emptiness and loneliness. This persistent desire for change cultivates feelings of anger, frustration, resentment, and self-pity, contributing to a cycle of chronic negative emotions.

An example of chronic wishing is wishing that your childhood, your parents, or your past would be different. You may not realize that all the adversity and the absence of love and attention contributed to building the strengths and resilience you now possess. Nevertheless, by fixating on what you wish were different, you remain stuck in a cycle of longing and wanting. This harmful energy prevents you from being open to new possibilities and opportunities that the universe has in store for you.

As you can see, the harmful energy driving your behaviors has consequences. These consequences include negative impacts on your curiosity, creativity, goal achievement, productivity, relationships, capacity for love and kindness, and empathy. Ultimately, they lead to a profound sense of disconnection from your authentic self. By mindfully becoming aware, without judgment or shame of your behaviors and actions, you will gain insight into their origins and underlying motives. While this awareness can be painful, it is essential for improving your emotional and spiritual health.

To bring about any desired change to your harmful energy states, it is essential to start by observing how you relate to yourself and how you interact with the world. When you confront your reality, it can be painful and perhaps even scary, which is why we often avoid change and remain in self-destructive behaviors. When you become aware of the changes you need to make in your life, the next step is to set an intention.

The Seat of the Soul author Gary Zukav defines intention as the quality of consciousness that infuses your thoughts, emotions, and actions with purpose and direction. It is the energy behind your choices and decisions that is shaping your experiences. He explains that consequences are the natural outcomes or results of the intentions that we set, and every intention, whether conscious or unconscious, generates its own set of consequences.

"Intentions are the invisible but potent forces that shape our lives. They set the course for our actions and determine our outcomes."
~ Steven Pressfield, The War of Art

How does harmful energy infiltrate my life?

~ 4 ~

CULTIVATING THE 3GS

The concept of the 3Gs—gratitude, gratefulness, and graciousness—serves as the focal point of this book, encapsulating a wholistic approach to cultivating kindness, appreciation, reverence, and compassion, all of which are needed for well-being.

Zen Master Brother Phap Huu explains that understanding is at the heart of practicing the 3Gs. It involves being open to the full spectrum of human experiences, including suffering, both your own and that of others. Rather than avoiding or denying the complexities of life, embracing understanding allows you to shift from a mindset of fear to one of love. This enables you to act from a place of compassion and empathy towards yourself and others.

Brother Phap Huu emphasizes the karmic nature of an understanding practice, suggesting that it not only heals the wounds of the past but also honors our heritage and the contributions of our ancestors, whose actions paved the way for our existence in the present moment.

Engaging in the practice of the 3Gs throughout your life serves as a remedy for loneliness and separateness. It offers a path towards developing stronger connections with yourself and others to live an intuitive and soulful life amidst challenges of the external world.

Cultivating the 3Gs encourages you to cease running from your trauma, pain, and suffering and instead embracing them as integral parts of our journey towards self-discovery of your strengths, worthiness, and wholeness. These qualities—gratitude. gratefulness, and graciousness —are intricately linked to resilience, the capacity to rebound from adversity. Moreover, they serve as pillars for nurturing empathy, compassion, spiritual flourishing, and healthy relationships that encompass broader implications for societal well-being.

Why is it important to me to cultivate a 3G practice in my life?

~ 5 ~

ABSENCE OF THE 3GS

The absence of regular practice of the 3Gs—gratitude, gratefulness, and graciousness—can lead to significant suffering and disconnection from life's inherent abundance. Buddhist philosophies explain that without cultivating these qualities, you may experience a sense of dissatisfaction and lack (dukkha) that impede genuine happiness and well-being (sukha).

Omitting a 3G practice can also lead to unawareness of life's blessings and the interconnectedness of all beings (avidya), contributing to feelings of separateness and isolation (anatta). Additionally, a lack of loving-kindness and compassion towards oneself and others (metta) strains feelings of belonging and understanding and perpetuates loneliness and suffering.

Without the 3Gs, you may find yourself focusing more on the negative aspects of your life, which can lead to chronic anxiety and feelings of hopelessness, depression, and unworthiness. Dwelling on what is lacking or what has gone wrong in your life can create a cycle of deficit thinking, generating harmful energy and activating unintended emotions and behaviors that exacerbate mental health issues.

Neglecting to cultivate the 3Gs throughout your life can have significant consequences as you reach your senior years. Reflecting back on your life, you may experience profound regret and even severe depression as consequences of choosing fear over courage to become 3G adapted.

What prevents me from cultivating a daily 3G practice?

Draw something from deep within my soul.

~ 6 ~
GRATITUDE & GRATEFULNESS

Gratitude and gratefulness are distinct yet interconnected concepts. Gratitude typically involves acknowledging and appreciating the specific actions or contributions of others towards our well-being, even if we feel undeserving. In contrast, gratefulness is a broader sense of thankfulness for favorable circumstances or states of affairs, often without attributing them to a particular individual or entity.

While gratitude is directed towards someone, gratefulness emphasizes what we are thankful for, regardless of whether there is a specific agent to whom gratitude is owed. Additionally, gratefulness can extend to inanimate objects or aspects of our natural environment that provide us nourishment, resources, or a sense of awe. Gratefulness enables a deeper emotional experience and appreciation.

Most use gratitude and gratefulness interchangeably, defining them as the act of acknowledging and deeply appreciating the kindness and abundance bestowed upon us. Using them interchangeably is generally acceptable because they are closely related terms that convey similar meanings. Both words refer to the quality of being thankful or appreciative and are expressed to produce a sense of connection and belonging.

Examples of Gratitude and Gratefulness

Gratitude

- Picture yourself facing a difficult period in your life, and a friend dedicates their time listening to you, providing unwavering support, and guiding you through your struggles. You feel a profound sense of gratitude as you realize the depth of their kindness. You appreciate the impact their actions have on your well-being, and you are truly thankful for their presence and support during this challenging time.

- Envision a world where no one tended to the upkeep of public spaces like bathrooms and kitchens. Consider the tireless efforts of janitors, cleaners, and maintenance workers who diligently ensure these areas remain sanitary and functional for everyone's benefit. When you embrace gratitude, you have the power to reframe your outlook and appreciate these unsung heroes who often go unnoticed yet play a crucial role in maintaining the cleanliness and hygiene of our shared environments.

- Picture a soldier deployed overseas, far from the comforts of home. They endure long stretches of time away from loved ones, facing the harsh realities of combat and the toll it takes on their mental and physical well-being. Despite these challenges, their sense of duty remains steadfast. In recognizing and expressing gratitude for their service, we acknowledge the sacrifices they make and the risks they undertake on behalf of our country.

This appreciation not only lifts their spirits but also strengthens our collective sense of solidarity and support for those who serve and their families.

Gratefulness

- As the sun dips below the horizon, you find solace in the quiet stillness of nature. Surrounded by the beauty of the outdoors, you take a moment to pause and reflect. The gentle rustle of leaves and the soft chirping of birdsong provide a comforting backdrop, grounding you in the present moment. In this tranquil setting, you cannot help but feel a sense of gratefulness for the peacefulness and serenity that nature generously offers.

- Experiencing the warmth and security of your home can evoke a profound sense of gratefulness for the fundamental necessities and comforts that often go overlooked. This feeling of gratefulness nurtures a deeper appreciation for the privileges and opportunities afforded to you.

- As you gather around the dinner table with loved ones, laughter and conversation fill the air. Each smile, each shared story, and each moment of connection reminds you of the depth of relationships in your life. In this shared space, surrounded by warmth and familiarity, you feel grateful for the bond that unites you with family and friends, creating a sense of belonging and love that enriches your life in many countless ways.

~ 7 ~
GRATITUDE & GRATEFULNESS PRACTICES

In what ways do I express gratitude and gratefulness? Why is this important to me?

How will practicing gratitude help me feel more connected to others?

How will gratefulness help me feel more connected to my environment and my privileges?

Spend some time observing my environment without judgements, labels, or opinions. Describe what I see and what it is like to be the observer.

In what areas of my life do I feel cultivating a 3G practice will be most helpful?

Take some time to capture visions by paying close attention to them. Translate these experiences into a drawing to visually express what I am experiencing.

~ 8 ~

FINDING MEANING

The philosophy of finding meaning addresses the fundamental questions surrounding human existence, purpose, accomplishment, and fulfillment. Rooted in existentialist and philosophical traditions, meaning asserts that individuals hold the agency to create significance in one's life. There is a subjective nature to meaning, proposing that purpose is not predefined but rather constructed through personal experiences, choices, and values.

Finding meaning goes beyond the ego, beyond superficial wants, and taps into the essence of what truly matters to you. Whether through personal relationships, meaningful work, curiosity, discovery, or spiritual connection, having an intention for finding meaning provides a compass to guide your actions and decisions. By cultivating the 3Gs, you enrich your journey towards a more meaningful and purposeful life, aligning your values, aspirations, and actions with what truly matters to you.

Existential philosophers like Jean-Paul Sartre and Viktor Frankl have explored how individuals can find profound meaning by taking responsibility and accountability for one's life. Being responsible and accountable takes courage, as it requires confronting challenges while acknowledging and working with the fear that accompanies these endeavors. The process of finding meaning requires self-observation, reflection, contemplation, intention, conscious living, and having knowledge of your values.

Finding meaning gives you a sense of purpose and a feeling of accomplishment in the unfolding narrative of your existence.

As you engage with the meaning-pondering questions on the next several pages, allow your soulful thoughts to flow onto the page. Make it a ritual to build and sustain a regular mindful practice, deliberately choosing varied responses each time. Resist the urge to label your thoughts and responses as right or wrong, good or bad, and approach these exercises without judgment or opinion. Embrace the evolving nature of your responses, allowing for deeper insight and understanding of yourself as you develop a brighter outlook on life.

~ 9 ~

MEANINGFUL PRACTICES

What is it about my family that makes me feel grateful?

What went pleasingly well during the past week, and why?

I have gratitude for (name a person). Why?

I am grateful for (name a thing). Why?

I am grateful for who I am. Why?

What silly thing am I grateful for? Why?

I am grateful because I accomplished _____ in the past week. Why is this meaningful to me?

Think about a fond memory. Why is this meaningful to me?

What is a difficult lesson I have learned recently? In what ways is this meaningful to me?

What am I excited about? Why?

Describe a random of kindness I witnessed or experienced. How did it impact me?

What would I not want to live without? Why?

When I receive genuine support or encouragement from someone, they believe in me. How does that feel? Why?

What do I wish for other people? Why?

Draw something that has meaning to me.

~ 10 ~
"I GET TO!"

The "I Get To!" practice is designed to shift your mindset from harmful energy to healthy and inspiring energy. The idea is to change your mindset from dreading and complaining to an "I get to!" mindset. An "I get to!" mindset helps you recognize your privileges, abundance, and blessings.

"I Get To!" is a powerful gratitude practice designed to combat the negative energy state that you consciously and unconsciously create within yourself. By shifting your mindset from dread and complaining to gratitude, you will transform your internal landscape into one of inspiration and contentment. This shift is fundamental in changing your perspective about your circumstances and recognizing the privileges you have that are often taken for granted.

The essence of "I Get To!" lies in its capacity to reshape your thoughts, perceptions, and emotions. For instance, instead of grumbling about going to work, you can alter your mindset to value the chance to earn income, pay bills, support loved ones, grow professionally, and contribute to the greater good.

Similarly, rather than procrastinating on household chores, you can view them as opportunities to express creativity, show self-kindness, and cultivate serenity in your living space.

By consciously annd intentionally adopting an "I Get To!" mindset, you invite optimism and joy into your heart, thus creating a ripple effect of happiness and fulfillment into your demeanor and everyone you touch.

"It's a funny thing about life, once you begin to take note of the things you are grateful for, you begin to lose sight of the things that you lack."
~ Germany Kent

~ 11 ~
"I GET TO!" PRACTICES

Take a moment to write down five or more activities, people, or things that you often find yourself dreading or complaining about. It may require several weeks or even months of consistent observation to fully acknowledge how frequently you engage in blame, shame, complaint, and judgment.

Next, take some time to reflect on *why* you are grateful for the privileges and opportunities that you have the chance to experience.

For instance: I do not particularly enjoy mowing the lawn. As I prepared to mow for the first time this spring, I noticed a sense of dread creeping in. Recognizing this feeling, I consciously shifted my mindset. I reminded myself, *"I get to mow the lawn. I'm grateful for having a lawn to maintain. Many people wish for a nice yard like mine. So, I feel privileged and deeply grateful :-)."*

This exercise is not about whether you like or dislike the tasks you have to do. Instead, it is about bringing awareness to your unconscious tendency to generate chronic, self-induced negative energy—a feeding ground for the ego, the part of the self that is driven by self-importance and the need for validation, rather than support for the soul. The objective is to develop self-awareness regarding how often you contribute to your own suffering and embrace a "Poor me" mindset. Don't let this be your Karma!

Examples of "I Get To!" Practices

I dread this cold, damp, and dreary weather.
I get to I live in an area full with diverse and stunning natural landscapes, including lakes, mountains, waterfalls, wildlife, and flowers, all because of the weather conditions.

I dread having to do and keep up with laundry.
I get to have clean clothes that are organized and easy to access, and this makes me feel good.

I dread having to spend time with _____.
I get to learn from this person how to be open-minded, patient, and maybe even appreciate their presence while also setting necessary boundaries for my safety and well-being.

I dread getting out of bed this morning to hike in this 40° drizzle.
I get to have the privilege of exercising because I make it a time priority. I am grateful for my physical ability to hike and appreciate living in a safe and beautiful area where the morning views are simply amazing.

I dread my job.
I get to create opportunities to explore new career and education paths to find more fulfilling and soul-enriching work.

I dread being in school.
I get to have the opportunity to maximize my education because it opens doors to countless opportunities and unexpected possibilities.

These examples are highly customizable to your life situations. If you are struggling to get started, pay attention to how often you find yourself dreading or complaining about a specific topic, person, or place. Then consciously shift your mindset to focus on how and why you are grateful for the opportunities, blessings, and privileges you possess.

Write down 5 or more activities, people, or things that I dread or complain about. Then rethink the dread and replace with the mindset "I get to!" Include the reasons why I have gratitude and am grateful.

Draw something that I am grateful for.

~ 12 ~
SELF-GRATITUDE

Self-gratitude is a lifelong practice wherein you acknowledge and appreciate yourself for who you are, what you have accomplished, and the journey you are on—*without judgment or shaming*. It involves cultivating a deep sense of appreciation and kindness towards yourself, regardless of perceived failures or shortcomings. Self-gratitude acknowledges your soul, your worthiness, and your genius. Establishing a healthy relationship with yourself is crucial for developing strong relationships with others because self-awareness and self-acceptance provide the foundation for empathy, understanding, and effective communication.

Self-gratitude involves recognizing and celebrating your small victories, milestones, accomplishments, and moments of growth in life. It means that you acknowledge the efforts you have made and will continue to make, the challenges you have overcome, the resilience you have demonstrated, and the lessons learned from failures. It is having clear goals for your well-being and kindly understanding that you are a lifelong work-in-progress. Embracing your new self-gratitude practice helps you connect deeper with your intuitive self, motivating greater self-awareness, self-acceptance, self-kindness, and self-worth.

Practicing self-gratitude involves intentionally taking time to list and reflect on your strengths, your graciousness, and the joy of simply being. It includes regularly writing about your gratitude or finding other creative ways to express what truly matters. Engaging in self-gratitude and self-kindness develops a deeper connection with your instinctual nature, which is too often ignored, and helps you maintain boundaries with those who project their negative and harmful energy onto you.

In Buddhist philosophy, self-gratitude emanates from the practice of loving-kindness and compassion toward yourself, known as "Metta" or "Maitri." It involves recognizing and honoring your inherent worthiness and uniqueness as a sentient being (an organism capable of experiencing sensations and feelings) on the path of becoming consciously aware. Self-gratitude is rooted in the understanding of "Anatta," the concept of non-self, which teaches that if you have sense of a separate, permanent self, it is an illusion.

The 3G practices teach us that there is an interdependent web of existence, where all beings are interconnected and deserving of love and kindness, especially with oneself.

~ 13 ~

SELF-DEPRECATION

Self-deprecating language can have a humorous effect, and its use can bond or connect us with others. It can be used to share one's humanity and humility through conversation, a speech, a comedic skit, or an anecdotal story. However, self-deprecation most often manifests as a harmful energy state.

Self-deprecation represents the antithesis of a self-gratitude practice by embodying the act of belittling or undervaluing yourself. It includes downplaying your abilities, worth, and accomplishments. Self-deprecation may serve as a defense mechanism to cope with fear, insecurity, or to appear more relatable and approachable to others. However, excessive self-deprecation can have detrimental effects by repeatedly reinforcing negative self-perceptions.

Unfortunately, self-deprecation is frequently viewed as culturally appropriate, and it is often learned and modeled. These tendencies are typically acquired from observing family members, close friends, and peers practice forms of self-deprecation. You may also notice self-deprecation through sarcasm, where you make negative remarks or jokes about your abilities, appearance, or character traits. Moreover, media and popular culture can influence self-deprecating behaviors through characters in movies and television, as well as social media influencers who use self-deprecating humor for relatability or entertainment, thereby normalizing this behavior.

While occasional self-deprecating humor can be lighthearted and relatable, chronic self-deprecation erodes your self-worth and reinforces a negative self-image. Constantly downplaying achievements or deflecting compliments undermines your confidence, growth, and goals.

How to Recognize Self-Deprecating Behaviors

Labels ~ Referring to yourself with derogatory labels such as "stupid," "ugly," or "lazy" can have profound and damaging effects on agency (the capacity to act independently and make free choices), authenticity, confidence, and capabilities. Using derogatory labels to describe yourself can also influence how others perceive and interact with you, reinforcing negative perceptions and potentially attracting abusive relationships. This negative self-labeling can limit personal growth and achievement by discouraging you from pursuing opportunities that truly feed your soul due to self-imposed and imaginary limitations.

Language ~ Using harmful language and a negative "tone," oftentimes accompanied by an eye roll, can significantly impact your self-perception. For instance you might say something like, *"I always seem to mess things up. I can never get anything right,"* or more sarcastically, *"Oh, great, I've managed to spill coffee on myself again. I'm clearly a master of coordination."* This habitual behavior often occurs without awareness, and you may not realize the impact this unkindness has on your self-confidence.

Actions ~ Harmful behaviors towards youself can encompass a range of actions or inactions that negatively impact physical, mental, and emotional well-being. Several examples of such behaviors include:

- *Procrastination* ~ Putting off important tasks or responsibilities repeatedly leads to increased anxiety, depression, and a sense of inadequacy.

- *Substance Use* ~ Consuming substances such as alcohol or drugs in excessive quantities or with high frequency wastes a significant amount of time that could be better spent on more productive activities.

- *Irregular Sleep Schedule* ~ Not maintaining a consistent sleep routine, either with too much or too little sleep, can lead to fatigue, moodiness, overeating, grogginess, and poor cognitive functioning.

- *Eating Processed Foods* ~ Consuming high amounts of processed or unhealthy foods contributes to nutrient deficiencies, weight gain, lethargy, feelings of self-loathing, and an increased risk of chronic diseases.

- *Lack of Movement* ~ Failing to engage in regular exercise and stretching leads to weakness, decreased flexibility, and an increased risk of cardiovascular and other health issues.

- *Ignoring Health Needs* ~ Neglecting to seek medical attention or mental health counseling for physical or psychological issues can keep you trapped in negative energy states and prevent you from living your best life.

- *Isolation or Neediness* ~ Engaging in extremes of social behavior, such as isolating yourself and neglecting your need for belonging, or being overly needy and disrespecting others' boundaries, can lead to damaged relationships, increased loneliness, and a weakened sense of self-worth.

- *Boundaries* ~ Failing to establish boundaries with individuals who are disrespectful or manipulative is a form of self-neglect. Opting to people please instead of setting boundaries can perpetuate feelings of guilt and shame, which in turn can contribute to feelings of anger or depression.

If you habitually engage in self-deprecating behavior, you may also find yourself dependent on seeking validation—the need for reassurance from others. This behavioral addiction manifests as a chronic seeking of external approval to counteract your feelings of inadequacy or self-doubt.

Furthermore, as we grow older, one of the most significant challenges many people encounter is reflecting on their lives and feeling regret over missed opportunities and things they didn't do. This sense of regret can stem from not pursuing passions, avoiding risks, or not taking advantage of opportunities that could have led to personal growth and a richer life.

To minimize these regrets, it is important to develop a 3G mindset that includes courage and curiosity. Choose to be kind, brave enough to pursue your passions, and open to new experiences.

In what ways do I treat myself poorly?

~ 14 ~

SELF-GRATITUDE PRACTICES

Although I am a work-in-progress, can I accept myself right now, just the way I am? Why or why not? How will I incorporate self-gratitude as a regular practice?

How will I incorporate self-gratitude as a regular practice?

Reflect on my accomplishments, big or small. Write down at least three achievements that I am proud of. For each accomplishment, reflect on the skills, qualities, or efforts that contributed to my success.

Think about the qualities, strengths, and attributes that I appreciate about myself. Write down at least three things that I admire or value about myself. These could be personality traits, talents, or characteristics that make me unique.

What are the positive qualities that other people would say that I have? Why would they say these things about me?

What boundaries do I need to establish with other people to protect my emotional, mental, and physical well-being? How would these boundaries contribute to my self-worth and self-respect?

What improvements do I need to make to prioritize my authenticity and self-worth?

Draw something that brings me a sense of delight.

~ 15 ~
GRACIOUSNESS

Graciousness refers to the quality of being courteous, kind, and considerate towards others. It goes beyond mere politeness, embodying a deep ethos of kindness, consideration, and empathy. Graciousness encompasses a genuine spirit of generosity and altruism, where acts of kindness are offered selflessly and without expecting reciprocation.

Practicing graciousness involves cultivating a mindset of optimism and understanding. It entails striving to elevate and support those around you, regardless of their circumstances or actions; however, you must also always prioritize your safety. Whether it is offering an ear to a friend in need, extending a helping hand to a stranger, or showing yourself compassion in moments of self-doubt, graciousness permeates every interaction and decision you make. It is a powerful force for connection and harmony in your relationships and community, reflecting a commitment to promoting a more compassionate and inclusive world.

There is a "ripple effect" quality to acts of graciousness that extends far beyond individual interactions, healthy relationships, and improving communities. When you choose to embody graciousness, you uplift those around you and serve as a positive and adaptive role model for others and future generations. By demonstrating kindness, empathy, and reverence in your actions, behaviors, and words, you have the power to inspire others to emulate these qualities.

Children, adolescents, and young adults who are regularly exposed to gracious behaviors learn valuable lessons about compassion, generosity, and interpersonal skills. As they carry forward these principles into adulthood, this propagates a culture of kindness and empathy that transcends time. In this way, the impact of graciousness extends through the years, influencing successive generations to prioritize empathy and understanding. Imagine how your practice of graciousness could change the world!

Examples of Graciousness in Action

Whether it is lending a loved one or a stranger a helping hand, offering a random act of kindness, providing genuine emotional support, or treating yourself with kindness, the act of intentionally expressing gratitude through graciousness and generosity signifies that you are recognizing and valuing the grace that has been placed your life.

Manners ~ Holding the door open for someone behind you, offering someone a seat, including someone who looks out of place in a conversation, using and remembering someone's name, saying "please" and "thank you."

Validation ~ Offering a sincere compliment to someone for something you have noticed or a job well done.

Offering assistance ~ When appropriate, helping others in need such as helping with chores or a specific job.

Forgiving ~ Forgiving someone for a mistake or misunderstanding lets them experience your empathy and understanding and encourages growth and change in their behavior.

Kind words ~ Offering words of encouragement or support to someone facing challenges helps them feel less alone in their struggles.

Respecting ~ Being open to opinions that differ from your own shows respect and provides an opportunity for learning and growth.

Verbal acknowledgement ~ Saying "thank you" and using eye contact amplifies sincerity and warmth to your expression of gratitude. Making eye contact while saying thank you helps to establish a positive connection between you and the other person, reinforcing the value of your appreciation and leaving a lasting impression of gratitude and sincerity.

Thank you notes ~ Sending a handwritten thank-you note or a thoughtfully written email expresses appreciation for someone's kindness, generosity, or assistance.

Acts of kindness ~ Performing acts of kindness to pay it forward can strengthen connections and nurture a sense of belonging for both yourself and others in your community.

Quality time ~ Spending quality time with someone, whether it is having a meaningful conversation, going for a walk together, or enjoying a meal, is helpful because it strengthens relationships and emotional connections.

Gift giving ~ Giving an appropriate and thoughtful gift shows how much you appreciate someone for their support or generosity.

Public acknowledgment ~ If appropriate, recognize someone's contributions or efforts publicly, such as in a meeting or gathering. It boosts the motivation of the individual, making them feel valued, and it inspires others to act kindly.

.

Compliments ~ Giving someone a genuine compliment validates their efforts, builds confidence, encourages personal growth, strengthens relationships, and promotes feelings of connectedness.

Reverence ~ is the daily practice of seeing life's sacredness from a place of humility and high regard. It is a regular practice of appreciation for the interconnectedness and inherent worth of all forms of life.

Proactive listening ~ This type of listening involves giving someone your focused attention by using nonverbal cues, reflecting back what the speaker says, expressing appropriate empathy, asking open-ended questions, avoiding interruptions, and summarizing key points. By actively engaging, it ensures effective communication, builds trust, and reduces misunderstandings.

Apologies ~ Taking the time to intentionally and genuinely acknowledge your mistakes and wrongdoings demonstrates that you have integrity, reverence, and empathy. Apologizing allows for reconciliation and helps repair damaged relationships.

Giving ~ Appropriate donations are acts of appreciation that have a meaningful impact on individuals and communities, encouraging feelings of connection and worthiness.

It is very important not to expect reciprocation when offering graciousness because true graciousness is about giving without attachment to receiving something in return.

When you offer graciousness with the expectation of getting something back, it will likely change the nature of your expression from genuine appreciation to a transactional exchange. This can create pressure or obligation on the recipient and may undermine the sincerity of your generosity.

Additionally, if you are expecting reciprocation, this can lead to disappointment or resentment if the other person does not respond in the way you anticipated. Graciousness is most meaningful when it is freely given from the heart and soul, without any strings attached.

~ 16 ~
MISUSE OF GRACIOUSNESS

Some harmful ways people may misuse graciousness include using it for personal gain, to alleviate guilt, or as a form of people-pleasing. Here are a several examples:

Manipulation can involve leveraging acts of kindness and generosity to control or influence others for personal gain or desires.

Insincerity is displaying graciousness or kindness insincerely, without genuine care or concern for others but rather as a facade to appear benevolent or gain favor. For instance, using social media to post acts of graciousness with the sole intention of gaining recognition and followers.

Emotional blackmail is guilt-tripping or emotionally manipulating others by emphasizing one's own graciousness or past favors to elicit certain behaviors or responses.

Alleviating guilt involves manipulating acts of kindness or generosity as a way to seek forgiveness or validation for one's own wrongdoing. This can manifest through over-apologizing or being excessively polite in an attempt to appease others and ease feelings of guilt. Additionally, seeking approval through excessive generosity or helpfulness may serve as a means of compensating for past actions or inadequacies.

Avoiding confrontation ~ Using graciousness as a way to avoid addressing conflicts or difficult conversations, thereby trying to maintaining harmony at the expense of genuine communication and resolution.

Enabling is continuously accommodating or appeasing others out of a sense of obligation or guilt, even when it is detrimental to your own well-being or your boundaries.

People pleasing is engaging in validation-seeking behaviors through excessive acts of graciousness in order to seek approval, validation, or acceptance from others, rather than acting intuitively and authentically.

These unkind and harmful behaviors can undermine the true essence of graciousness and lead to unhealthy dynamics in relationships. It is important to authentically express kindness and generosity that is rooted in empathy, compassion, and reverence for others' well-being, rather than using it as a tool for personal gain, neediness, or validation.

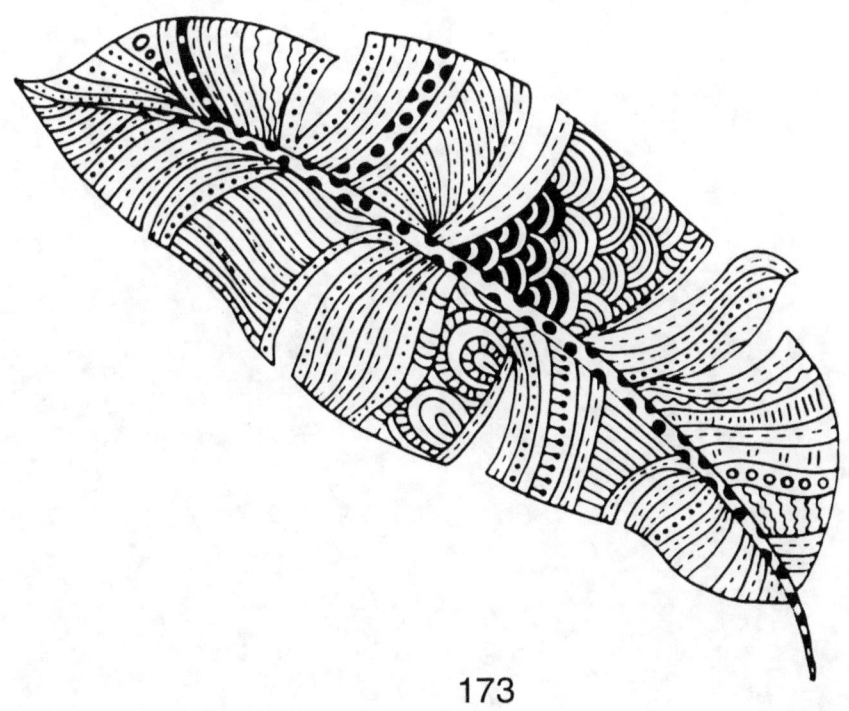

How have I misused graciousness?

~ 18 ~

GRACIOUSNESS PRACTICES

Listening to someone's story in a proactive manner. Write about it. What emotions do I notice evoked by their story? How would I express graciousness to the storyteller?

In what ways have I expressed graciousness to others without expecting reciprocation?

In what ways can I be more generous with others while ensuring my own safety and well-being?

How can I intentionally practice and express graciousness in my daily life?

How can I practice more graciousness in my online and social media presence?

Write down the story I tell myself in my thoughts. What feelings do I notice coming up as I am writing? How can I express graciousness to myself?

Think about a goal or aspiration. How can I pursue this goal with graciousness, patience, optimism, and understanding?

Reflect on a past conflict or disagreement I had with someone. How could I have handled the situation with more graciousness? What steps can I take to resolve conflicts more constructively in the future?

Think about a time when I received feedback or criticism from someone. How did I respond? Reflect on how I can show graciousness in receiving feedback, even when it's challenging.

Consider a person in my life who may be going through a difficult time. Brainstorm ways I can offer appropriate support or assistance to them, demonstrating graciousness and kindness.

When I am exposed to someone I do not like, think about ways I can see them in a different and compassionate light?

Draw a concept that represents graciousness and generosity.

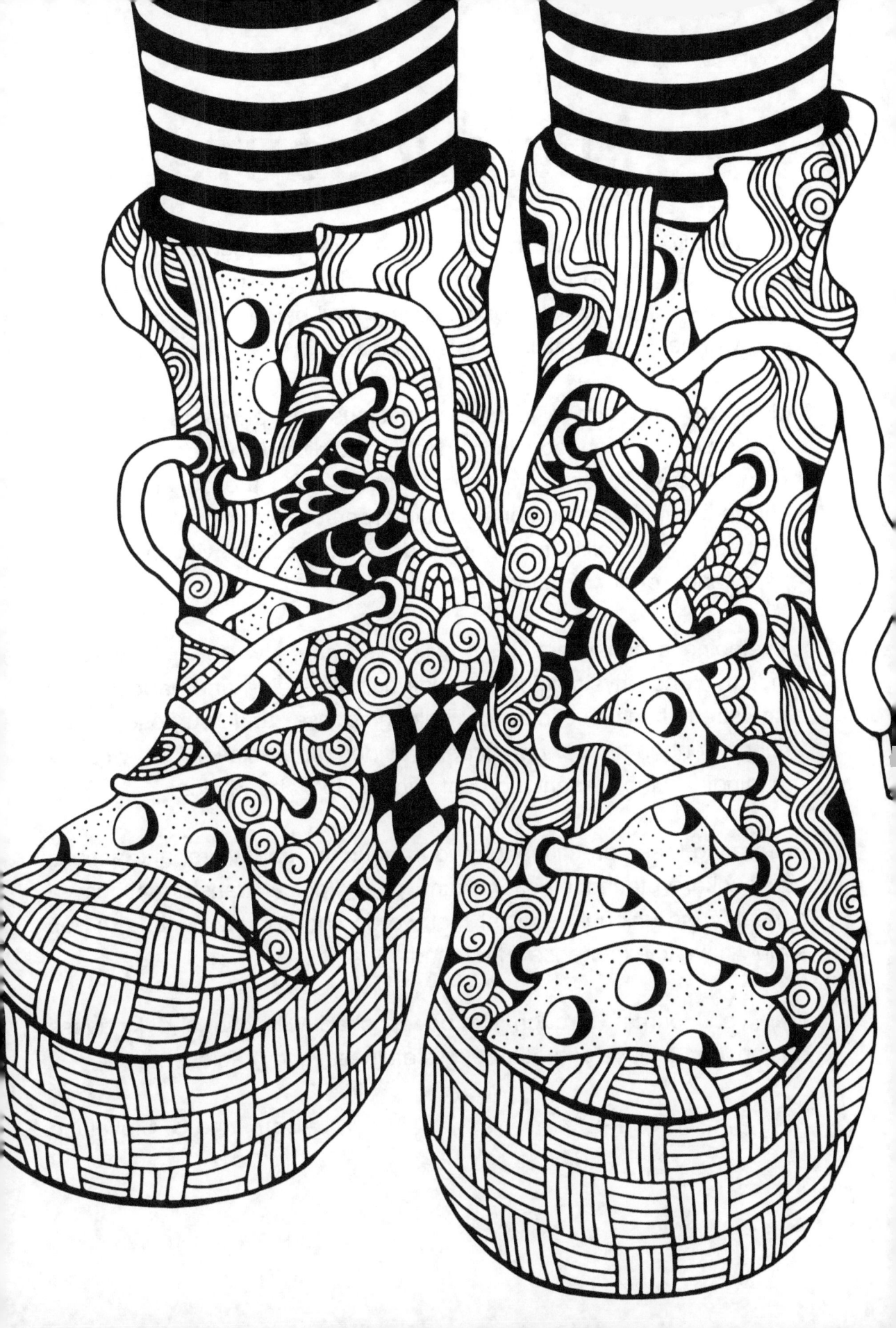

FINAL THOUGHTS

My objective in writing this book is to address some of the most common interventions used in my practice and present them in a guided format to assist those seeking well-being and finding their empowerment, authenticity, and self-worth.

Additionally, my aim is to raise conscious awareness regarding the various ways we engage in or become addicted to creating harmful energy states. These states often interfere with the development of intuitive and intimate personal and interpersonal relationships, as well as obstruct our ability to regain a deep connection with the healthy energy and wonder of nature.

Developing a consistent 3G practice is imperative for achieving an emotional and physiological shift in your well-being and happiness. It also strengthens feelings of belongingness and purpose. Daily engagement in these practices provides appreciation for what is meaningful in the present moment and for life's abundance.

Integrating these practices into your thoughts, behaviors, and actions can evoke profound emotional and physiological transformations—a sensation so uniquely special that words cannot fully capture it; you simply have to experience it firsthand.

May your journey through life be enriched will love and kindness arising from a place of gratitude, gratefulness, and graciousness.

~Catherine G. Cleveland

ACKNOWLEDGEMENTS

This book is a heartfelt tribute to the farmers, their families, and the other members of rural communities I serve who entrusted me with your mental health care. I extend my sincerest gratitude to each one of you for your trust and belief. Thank you!

I would like to express my heartfelt gratitude to peer counselor and advocate **Dawn Reckahn Stone** for the unwavering support, wisdom, and professional guidance that you have generously shared with me over the years. Your insights and expertise have been instrumental in shaping my personal and professional growth. However, beyond the realm of work, I am most grateful for the enduring friendship we have established. Your genuine kindness has given validation and meaning to my work and my life, and I treasure the wisdom we have cultivated together. Thank you for your continued friendship and support—I truly appreciate how special you are!

Thank you for reading!

CATHERINE'S NEWSLETTER

Join the Community for More Transformative Experiences!

Sign up today to unlock complimentary, practice-informed, and interactive resources focused on mental well-being. Be the first to learn about Catherine's latest books and public engagements, explore insightful articles in *The Wisdom Room* blog, and stay updated on all things mental health by subscribing to Catherine's Newsletter.

Get valuable insights and resources delivered straight to your inbox every month! Subscribe at:

www.catherinegcleveland.com/catherines-newsletter/

To find all of Catherine's interactive books on mental health, visit:

www.catherinegcleveland.com

To learn more about mental health counseling, visit:

www.clevelandemotionalhealth.com

Connect Catherine on Social Media:

Facebook ~ Catherine G. Cleveland

LinkedIn ~ Catherine G. Cleveland

Instagram ~ @CatherineGCleveland

X (Twitter) ~ @CatherineG.Clev

TikTok ~ CatherineGCleveland

www.ingramcontent.com/pod-product-compliance
Lightning Source LLC
Chambersburg PA
CBHW080839120626
46553CB00009B/2495